DEDICATION

I would like to dedicate this book to my children Ella & Elijas and all the wonderful friends who, over the years, have been a wonderful part of my life and who have inspired me.

Without your conscious support, I would have never written this book.

—Raschell Harlingten

Stand Tall In Your Truth

and

See Your Own Power

Raschell Harlingten is the founder of *Rooted For Success*, a personal development organization that helps individuals center and build strengths and success. She has also earned credentials as a transformational coach and speaker, and as a Real Estate Investor.

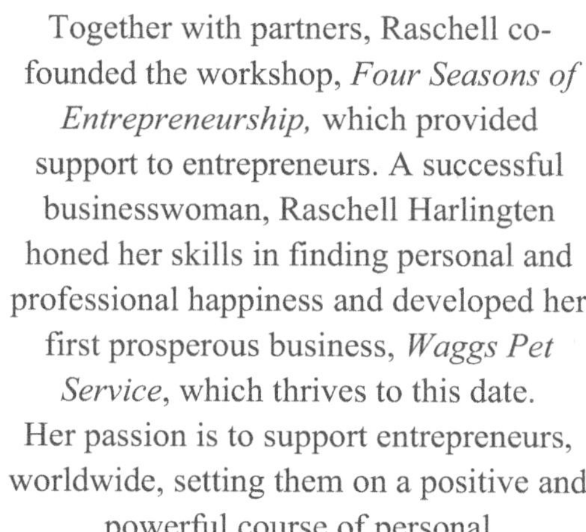

Together with partners, Raschell co-founded the workshop, *Four Seasons of Entrepreneurship,* which provided support to entrepreneurs. A successful businesswoman, Raschell Harlingten honed her skills in finding personal and professional happiness and developed her first prosperous business, *Waggs Pet Service*, which thrives to this date. Her passion is to support entrepreneurs, worldwide, setting them on a positive and powerful course of personal transformation that is critical to yielding success in business and in life. As a single mother of two children, she holds the empowerment of youth dear to her heart.

ISBN-978-1-77136-794-3

First printing, 2019

Publisher – Raschell Harlingten

Website : www.rootedforsuccess.com

Table of Contents

Foreword

Remember the way you felt as a child, holding a fluffy white dandelion and right before the moment of blowing all of the fluffy seeds, there was an incredible feeling of awe and wonder? You did not see this dandelion as a weed, it was instead so magical because all of its fluffy seeds could just fly away and be carried away by the wind, moving in many different directions. It is in these small moments that you were in the present moment, letting everything else go. As a child you had many of these moments, really being able to dive into your imagination and go anywhere, but as you grew older, many more rules and ways of acceptable behaviors came into place. You were told, you must do this or act this way to stay in alignment with what is acceptable.

We ask that you find you inner child and bring back those moments of being in the present and really nurture yourself on all levels. Allow yourself to slow down and savour each moment. Appreciate everything so fully with such awe and wonder. It is on this journey of going back to simplicity that you find yourself again, the core of your being, the essence of your true self.

I believe this books helps us remember who we are and find our true selves again in a truly magical way, catapulting us and empowering ourselves into creating such new and amazing possibilities in our lives.

—*Laura Master, Spiritual Designer*

Discovering Your Prosperity Blueprint

Stop looking at what you're going through.

Instead, look at how you're reacting to it.

As I walked through the arrival doors of the Toronto Pearson Airport with my friends and my daughter, a feeling of sadness and frustration washed over me. It was October and I had just come back from holiday in Costa Rica, I should have had feeling of happiness and peace, however I felt anxiety and I knew why. I was in denial and refusing to accept the feeling that was bubbling up inside of me.

I knew it was a pinnacle year of change and growth. In some ways, I had embraced it, however, I resisted accepting it.

I knew my marriage was over and I had to let go, my finances were in chaos, both of my vehicles had broken down three times and, to top it off, my teenaged daughter was struggling in school and in life. I realized that all things were happening for a reason and I could either rebel against all of this or embrace it all as a new beginning.

Decision rumbled inside me. As I rode quietly home in an Uber, the glittering lights of the city skyline reflecting in my car window, I decided that *I was not going to let myself be pushed by my past challenges, and rather be pulled by my vision for my future.* This decision represented a massive shift in thinking and the trajectory I would then create for myself.

It is all too easy to miss the bigger picture of what is trying to come through in our lives. We resent what we are experiencing, its difficulty, and we moor ourselves to the stress of it all. We ask *why me?* We have a thousand reasons as to why it should not be happening. But what we forget to look at, instead or first, is how *we react to it all*.

I was born in England and, at the age of four, my family began traveling where my father's work took us. We traveled to so many countries that, as small child, it was scary at times. However, I learned to adapt at a young age to differing customs and schools and became very good at blending in. I began to conform to opinions on how I was to present myself, what I was to say and how I was to act, based on where we were and who I was speaking to. At an early age, my blueprint was forming based on how I was expected to be.

By the time I was 15 years old, I had traveled to many countries—North Africa, Malta, New Zealand, Switzerland and Canada to name a few. During that time, I had also experienced many traumatic situations that left me with feelings and thoughts that were not my own but rather what I was told by society what was expected of me. As I reached my late teens, I began to rebel and ask why, and I refused to be told that this was the way it had to be, just because it was so.

The turning point for me was when I left North Africa for the last time and had been subject to the ridicule and inequity imposed on me, being a female and westerner.

When I arrived back in Canada in 1991, I was 23 years old and I fell into years of rebellion against imposed norms. My journey during that time was not an easy one. It was filled with despair frustration, lack of self-worth and suicidal thoughts. I abused drugs and alcohol to forget and pretend that nothing mattered. However, every now and then I would have moments where something within myself told me to keep going and not give up, even though I could not understand why or how I could keep going.

My first small steps to begin recognizing my story were terrifying, and at 39 years old, I walked away from a relationship of seven years, with my two small children in tow. Alone, scared and feeling hopeless, I knew in my heart that I could not let anyone tell me I would not succeed. I began to realize that my path in life—my success—was my own to create. However, I had to learn how to recreate the blueprint that had been imprinted on me by someone else's beliefs, and customs and the social paradigms I no longer wanted to follow.

In 2011 and at forty-five years old, I walked away from a corporate job with no idea how I was going to survive, let alone feed my children. But I held faith that something would show up, even when, in despair, I was forced to go to the local food bank to get food for my children. As I tucked my children in at night, I still believed something would change and that I would succeed. And I did: I built my first entrepreneurial business, going against everything and everyone's opinions and criticism and, to this day, the business is still thriving. These were my first steps in recreating.

Validating myself, and my purpose in life was my first goal. Understanding that, no matter what, looking outside of myself for validation from others would not help me grow.

Recognize that the stories we tell ourselves create our trajectory and the Blueprint for the basis of our life.

What story you tell yourself? When your day begins are you aware of how you feel, your thoughts, what you say out loud and what you visualize for your future?

Many people wake up with anxiety, regret and frustration over how they see what their lives have become. All of the early teachings and experiences we acquire piggyback into adulthood—good and bad. Some of which become our burdens.

As a parent I was always told what I should do, or should not do. At work I was told again how I should be and what I should say and how things were done. Even when talking to friends I was again told this is the way it is done. It was as if I had no options or free will.

Are your beliefs serving you? Or, are you letting others validate your feelings?

Are you setting your intention for the day or are you letting life happen to you? What are you telling yourself when things do not happen the way you expect them to? How do you react—with disappointment and self-reproach, or with acceptance and a positive way forward? You have the ability create a future based on what you wish to see and experience.

When you interact with family or friends, you make a conscious effort to engage in the positive and gently remove yourself from negative or critical conversations that do not inspire you or uplift you. Surround yourself with friends that welcome your achievements and accept your choices, whatever they may be, without judgement. Be aware of your feelings and what serves your highest good and what causes you to begin to criticize your beliefs or thoughts.

Look back as a child, even as early as 7-10 years of age. Look at what was articulated to us in school by teachers or peers our parents, TV social media. Children have purity and take everything to heart, if it comes from important people. Some of the people in a child's life are often flawed. The experiences children acquire can vary and most will carry the things that hurt them into adulthood. Mental, emotional, physical abuse, violence, neglect, criticism, unfairness and lack of advocacy, exploitation, expectations of others, to name a few.

As a child, we have limited tools to understand what serves us as we grow and mature. Sometimes we experience very traumatic or poignant situations in our life that leave us unsure of who we are and, for some, it feels arduous to come back from that experience. As we grow older, we being to question ourselves, second-guess our decisions and fall into social paradigms. However, is imperative to ask ourselves how we are reacting to situations. Are you beginning to formulate a *blueprint* that is serving your highest good? When we stop and have calm awareness of our experiences, we have made the first step in honouring ourselves.

Many of our influences have been passed down and we are told is this is just the way it is done.

I will share a common story.

One evening, a husband asked his wife *"why do you cut the ends of the ham off before you place it in the pot to cook"*. She replied *"I don't know. My mother always did, so I do."* The Husband replied *"can we call your mother? I want to know why."* They did call and her mother replied, *" I don't know. I have always done it because Grandmother did it."* This was passed down generationally because, as it turned out, her Grandmother cut off the ends so the ham would fit her pot.

Something that served your parents or grandparents or friends or their parents does not mean it serves you.

We begin to form a Blueprint based on what experiences or influences have been bestowed to us. Reflect on how those thoughts serve you, how they guide your life,

*and whether they help you achieve happiness
and fulfillment.*

How does telling ourselves a different story write a better *Blueprint* and improve our lives?

My first step in recreating my blueprint was to be aware of my first thoughts each day. I became keenly aware of what direction my thoughts took and began to change my focus from what was negative to what was positive and more aligned with my vision for my future.

Awareness is the first major step to rewriting any story. Awareness is hard and requires we stop, take ourselves out of the doing, and redirect our focus into our being. This was intrinsic in helping me stop looking at what I was going through, so that I could take an active role in changing my reactions. That switch in thinking and process is a monumentally different task that is rooted in a different goal and its outcome changes a person's trajectory, overall.

Each day's experiences got better.

Ask what's *right* and appreciate those things. Start small: the warm bed, soft pillow, food in your fridge, the singing of birds, the laughter of children, the freedom you have and being alive at this moment. Thoughts like this take you out of the past and bring you into the present. Acknowledging what we can be grateful for in the moment is -very powerful.

Once you have found small things to be grateful for, try to stay in the feeling of gratitude for as long as you can. Life will come at you with challenges, however starting off with gratitude and practicing that each day, you will be able to hold that feeling a little longer until you begin to find that waking up and embracing that feeling becomes your norm. *Changing your norm is life-altering: you've just changed the way you think.*

One thing that helped me was to write down my thoughts and feelings, together with the change I wanted to bring into my life. When you put pen or pencil to paper, you create a new Blueprint.

Having a daily journal or book to write down what you want to come into your life, what you want to see and how you want it unfold sets intention. So many people balk at this idea, saying it is waste of time. However, you are creating your life—your *masterpiece.*

Remember to focus positively on what you do want, versus what you don't want. Focus on what you see happening in our life, what you see creating itself, seeing the happiness, the joy, the success and the gratitude.

Begin to practice awareness of your thoughts each day. We have thousands of thoughts so, be aware of the string of negative thoughts and when you catch yourself, be happy for your car or your dog, or even that cup of coffee, or the smile of little child's face as they look at the world with happiness and excitement.

Before you close your eyes at night, think of what you want to bring into your life and stay in that positive place as you fall asleep. From there you gain access to all that you desire.

Enhance Your New Blueprint

Honour yourself. Be Present

On this journey, I realized that I had to be a bit selfish and make sure that I gave myself time to be with myself in peace. I took time to do things that I enjoyed and which made me happy, alone or with other people, to honour myself. For me painting, yoga and watching the waves roll in on the beach with my favorite Organo™ coffee and my dog were rejuvenating. These things also put me in the moment. No reflection, no thoughts, other than how Now is perfect when I see that it is.

Honour yourself. Be present. Make a conscious effort to bring your thoughts back to the now, in gratitude. This is very difficult for many of us. Our busy lives take us out of that mindset.

I also realized that becoming emotionally drawn-in when hearing others complain about their lives did not support me. I listened and was present and, only when they asked for support or advice did I offer neutrally. Listening is the best help we can give, or we end up fueling emotional *reactions* within us both.

When we listen with neutrality and honour, your outlook on the world beings to change.

As we begin to recognize our story and have awareness of what we say and think, we then need to look within ourselves for answers, which are all there. We just are so consumed by our day-to-day life and busy schedules that we tend not to take the time to quiet the busy mind.

Let's start with being aware of our Five Senses.

Many people have a hard time meditating or quieting their minds. Yet, others can do this with ease. It really depends on the individual. What I say is being present a little each day is like meditating and being present with our five senses of *touch, taste, hearing, smell* and *sight.* Let me share with you a few examples from my life.

After a very busy day at work, I came home to all my children wanting my attention and my phone was buzzing away. Before I let myself succumb to the circumstances of not knowing how to deal with it all at once, I proceeded to walk into the kitchen and began to wash dishes. I asked the children to give me a minute and I would address each of their concerns. As I washed the dishes, I watched the bubbles form and fade away, and looked at their rainbow colours through the sunlight from the window. Being present with what I saw and how the warm water felt on my hands, the sound of the water running on the dishes and the smell of the fragrant smell of apple from the dish soap. My state of overwhelm began to fade and a state of calmness began to envelope me. My fight or flight feeling had vanished and I was internally calm. I dried my hands and proceeded down the hall to address their concerns, feeling better equipped to deal with the challenges at hand. That simple exercise of washing dishes and being present with the bubbles the sunlight how the water felt on my hands and the sounds of the water brought me to the present moment so I was able to remove myself emotionally and respond calmly. Being present with my senses internally re-centered me.

Another example.

One day, I received a phone call that was very upsetting. The person on the other end was angry and shouting and I could feel I was being drawn into it. However, at that moment, I stopped reacting and just listened, even though it was challenging. Once the call was over, I sat there feeling upset and discordant. Then I turned my attention to the fresh coffee beside me, I closed my eyes and began drinking it. I appreciated the flavours, the warmth of the liquid going down my throat and the feeling of satisfaction of this hot beverage. I again focused my attention on my sense of smell, the taste, and the warm cup touching my hand, and the sounds around me. My feelings of hurt and frustration began to subside and my focus was solely on my coffee in that moment. My mind began to clear and my emotional state shifted.

Another example.

One day as I was driving to a client's house and realized that each way I drove, the streets was either blocked or heavily congested. I knew that this would delay me quite considerably. As I sat in my car, feelings of frustration began to boil up and negative thoughts began to form and the negative speak was emerging " *Gosh I am stupid. I should not have taken this route. I should have left earlier."* As I sat in my car, I turned my attention to children across the road as they played in the park and began to watch them so innocently chase each other, and the smiles on their faces. I was once again aware of my senses as I sat there feeling the warmth of the sun on my face, the smell of the spring air, the sounds of the children and the taste of the peppermint gum I was chewing. At that moment, I felt blessed to witness this tiny moment of joy. My anger at myself and the situation began to fade. As I glanced back at the traffic, I noticed the truck had moved and the traffic was beginning to move slowly. I could not control the traffic but I could control my thoughts so I made the conscious decision to shift my thinking.

In theses three examples, I was present in my senses and became less emotionally involved in situations that were not serving my highest good.

In the three examples, I mentioned self-talk, which is very powerful, whether it is negative or positive. We all do it in some way or other, however being aware of it is very important. What we think shifts our trajectory, however what we speak, we speak into existence.

Here is a daily exercise.

Your throat is the energy center in the body. Here, all changes take place. Touch your throat with your hand. When you speak, feel the vibration against your hand. When you touch your throat as you speak, you are acknowledging you are changing, and you wish to bring it into the now!

So let's begin, take a deep breath in and release two or three times slowly, while you close your eyes and say these five simple words "*I am willing to change.*" Then be aware of what feelings come up and what images form in your mind. Some of them may not be things you want to confront but be aware that the area where you do not want to change is exactly where you need to change the most.

Even though this exercise is simple, it is very powerful and these are simple examples but they are highly effective. When we practice them, they serve us well.

How does your new *Blueprint* change and inspire your life?

So let's first review if we have begun to be aware of what are our limiting beliefs are, and then apply them within the five areas of our lives: the Financial, Physical, Relational, Spiritual and Emotional areas. The beauty and joy of this progression is your focus of this exploration on how you can change your *Blueprint* in each of these areas, with conscious awareness. How is your day unfolding in these areas, and what is changing?

Setting your intention for each new day, what do you recognize is starting to change? When faced with challenges, are you able to see that change is happening in how you embrace it? Do you realize that how you react will bring about what you either want or do not want?

Each day brings us something new. We can be motivated even in the most uninspired moments. What *inspires* you each day now?

What goals have you set forth? Not only long-term goals but also daily goals that help you move forward towards your vision?

How are you validating yourself each day and what simple things are motivating you?

Are you aware of what is manifesting in your life and are you aware of the changes that brings?

Are you aware of how people are reacting to you, and the choices you make?

How are your reactions affecting your Emotional *wellbeing*?

How are your choices affecting you, Financially?

Are your Relationships serving your highest good?

Are you honouring your Physical being?

Are you taking the time to connect with your Spirituality?

Are you creating your new *Blueprint* and being pulled by your new visions for tomorrow?

My life now has changed so much that, at times, I do not even recognize it. But I know one thing for sure: my Blueprint serves my needs, and it creates the future I want.

I am no longer a prisoner of my thoughts. I am the master of my mind.

With much love, may you create your life, fully quenched, while standing tall in your truth.

—Raschell Harlingten

Gratitude -Notes